CITY BY NUMBERS

Stephen T. Johnson

PUFFIN BOOKS

To the memory of my grandfather

John Theodore Johnson

whom I knew only through his beautiful drawings and paintings,
which in turn nurtured my passion for art

PUFFIN BOOKS
Published by the Penguin Group
Penguin Putnam Books for Young Readers,
345 Hudson Street, New York, New York 10014, U.S.A.
Penguin Books Ltd, 80 Strand, London WC2R 0RL, England
Penguin Books Australia Ltd, 250 Camberwell Road, Camberwell, Victoria 3124, Australia
Penguin Books Canada Ltd, 10 Alcorn Avenue, Toronto, Ontario, Canada M4V 3B2
Penguin Books (N.Z.) Ltd, 182-190 Wairau Road, Auckland 10, New Zealand
Penguin Books Ltd, Registered Offices: Harmondsworth, Middlesex, England

First published in the United States of America by Viking, a member of Penguin Putnam Books for Young Readers, 1998
Published by Puffin Books, a division of Penguin Putnam Books for Young Readers, 2003

7 9 10 8 6

Copyright © Stephen T. Johnson, 1998
All rights reserved

THE LIBRARY OF CONGRESS HAS CATALOGED THE VIKING EDITION AS FOLLOWS:
Johnson, Stephen, date.
City by numbers / Stephen T. Johnson.
p. cm.
Summary: Paintings of various sites around New York City—from a shadow on a building to a wrought-iron gate
to the Manhattan Bridge—depict the numbers from one to twenty-one.
ISBN 0-670-87251-2 (hc)
1. Counting—Juvenile literature. [1. Counting. 2. New York (N. Y.)—Pictorial works.] I. Title.
QA113.J64 1998 513.2'11—dc21 98-20391 CIP AC
Puffin Books ISBN 0-14-056636-8
Printed in the United States of America
Set in Berthold Bodoni Antiqua

The paintings for this book were created with watercolors,
gouache, pastels, and charcoal on hot pressed watercolor paper.

AUTHOR'S NOTE

City by Numbers reflects my continuing attraction to cities for their wealth of visual possibilities. In these urban landscapes are wonderful images waiting to be transformed into paintings.

The idea for a number book evolved naturally while I was looking for letter shapes for my book *Alphabet City*. Inevitably I came upon urban subjects that resembled not only letters but numbers as well. Following the blueprint I created for *Alphabet City*, I have retained my various themes and self-imposed guidelines. Each image must be found in its natural position, out-of-doors or in a public space, readily accessible to anyone who looks carefully at our urban world at various times of day and during the cycle of the seasons.

One of the more interesting questions that arose in creating a number book was deciding where to stop. It was important that the numbers be sequential. A traditional number series might run from one through ten or twelve, but given my desire to paint as many interesting pictures as possible, I found this amount limiting. Twenty was much closer to what I was looking for, but not quite right. Then it dawned on me. Why not go to twenty-one? I found this a particularly significant number as we enter the new millennium and the twenty-first century.

Cities are one of our greatest human assets, for they embody and embrace diversity, connecting us with our past and linking us to our future. As the twenty-first century unfolds, it may be an appropriate time to reflect on the past century with its prodigious urban achievements and ask ourselves how we can preserve buildings, neighborhoods, and areas that have unique character and charm. It is also a time to marvel at our innovations as we move into this wondrous new era.

I hope that my paintings in this book, as with *Alphabet City*, will inspire children and adults to look at their surroundings in a fresh and playful way. In doing so they will discover for themselves juxtapositions of scale, harmonies of shadows, rhythms, colorful patterns in surface textures, and joy in the most somber aspects of a city, by transcending the mundane and unearthing its hidden beauty.

Stephen T. Johnson
New York City

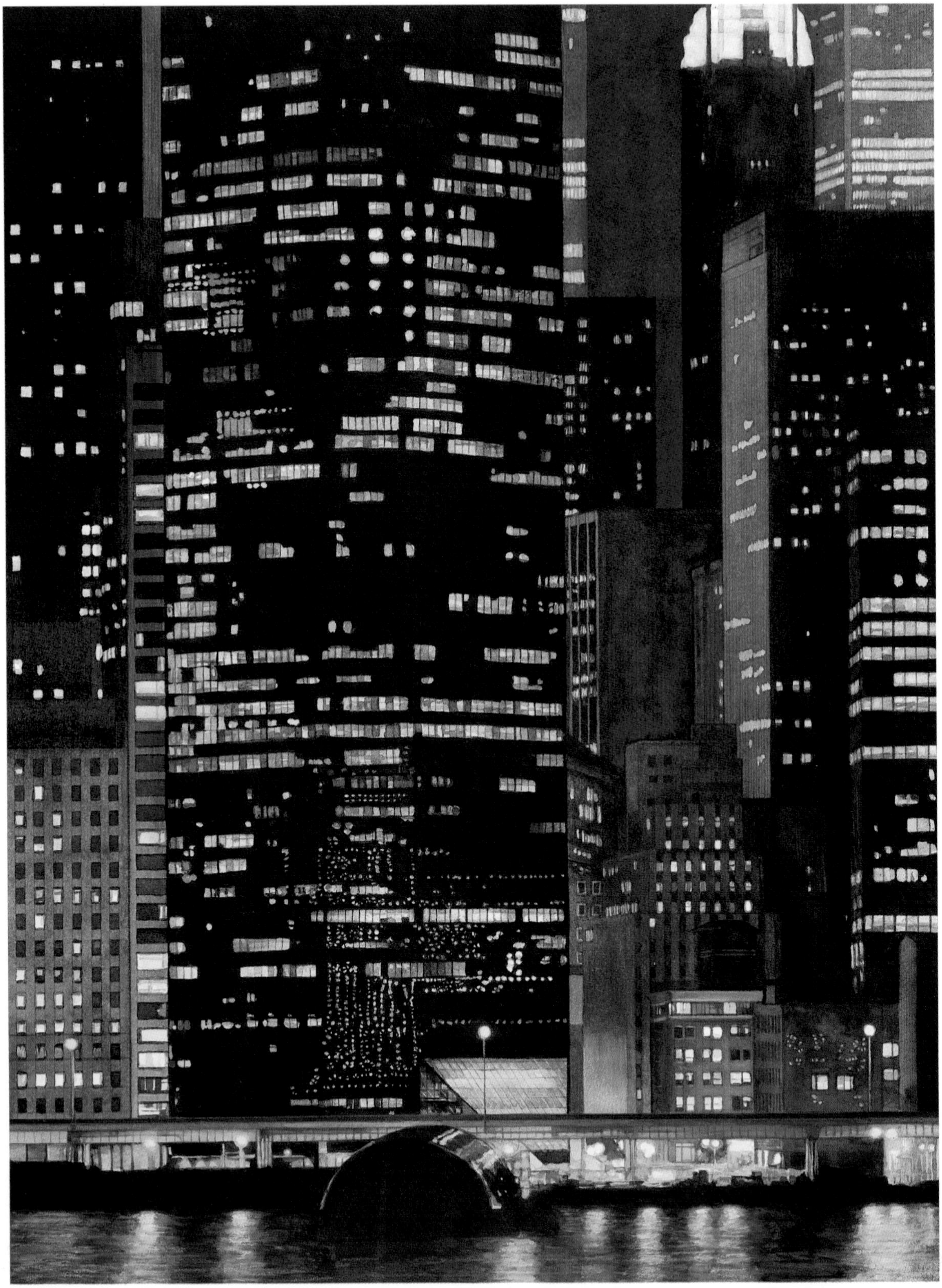